WITCHES AND WICCA

ELDORADO INK

THE SUPERNATURAL

Witches and Wicca

Haunted Places and Ghostly Encounters

New Orleans Voodoo

Shamans, Witch Doctors, Wizards, Sorcerers, and Alchemists

The Undead: Vampires, Zombies, and other Strange Monsters

Legendary Creatures

Unexplained Monsters and Cryptids

Angels, Demons, and Religious Rituals

THE SUPERNATURAL

WITCHES AND WICCA

BY AUDREY ALEXANDER

ELDORADO INK

Eldorado Ink
PO Box 100097
Pittsburgh, PA 15233
www.eldoradoink.com

Produced by OTTN Publishing, Stockton, New Jersey

CPSIA compliance information: Batch#S2015.
For further information, contact Eldorado Ink at info@eldoradoink.com.

First printing

1 3 5 7 9 8 6 4 2

Library of Congress Cataloging-in-Publication Data

Applied for
ISBN 978-1-61900-072-8 (hc)
ISBN 978-1-61900-080-3 (trade)
ISBN 978-1-61900-088-9 (ebook)

*For information about custom editions, special sales, or premiums,
please contact our special sales department at info@eldoradoink.com.*

TABLE OF CONTENTS

SORCERERS AT STONEHENGE

Deep in the heart of southern England stand 93 huge stones. Nobody knows who put them there, or what their purpose was. These enormous stones, some weighing more than 45 tons, have stood there for thousands of years, grouped together in a way that perfectly frames the sun on certain days of the year.

AN ANCIENT CIRCLE

The ancient circle is so precious that usually, visitors aren't permitted to walk next to them for fear that they'll damage the time-worn stones. Stonehenge is closed to the public, although visitors can access the stone circle if they receive permission in advance. On most days, only a few dozen visitors are allowed at the site each hour. But that all changes one day each year. During the Summer Solstice in June, Stonehenge opens for a special celebration. The night before the solstice, pilgrims start to arrive—tens of thousands of them.

On this day each year, up to 30,000 visitors are allowed to walk near the stones and come together in the middle of the massive circle.

Stonehenge, an ancient monument built by Stone Age people near Salisbury in the United Kingdom, has become a pilgrimage site for modern-day practicioners of neopagan religions, such as Wicca.

Every year, thousands of people gather at Stonehenge to observe and celebrate the Summer Solstice.

The Summer Solstice has more minutes of daylight than any other day in the year. It is also known as Midsummer. It usually occurs between June 20–22. The Wiccan holiday of Litha is celebrated during the Summer Solstice.

They're there to celebrate a sacred holiday, rain or shine. But who are the men and women who gather at Stonehenge every year? The answer is surprising.

That's because many of the people who make a point to gather at Stonehenge every summer are pagans, Druids, or witches. Wait...witches?! That's right. Witchcraft isn't just the stuff of movie magic...it's alive in modern culture.

THE WITCHES OF STONEHENGE

A person looking for a witch at Stonehenge during the Summer Solstice probably wouldn't recognize her. That's because modern witches don't wear pointy hats. They don't fly on brooms. And when

THE MYSTERY OF STONEHENGE

Stonehenge is so huge and so old that it can sometimes seem like an unsolvable mystery. Why was it built? Who built it? How did they do it? What does it mean? Even today, historians and archaeologists consider Stonehenge to be one of the most mysterious prehistoric sites.

Archaeologists have used modern scientific methods to research the Stonehenge site in an attempt to learn more about it. Most experts believe that it was probably built more than 5,000 years ago (about 3100 BCE). The area around Stonehenge does contain huge burial sites that include bones and ashes. But because Stonehenge was built by people who didn't write down their history, no one is certain how the enormous stones got to the site, or the purpose for which Stonehenge was built.

Even though modern scholars have been studying Stonehenge for many years, we're still learning more about its construction. In 2014, the people who maintain the site were watering the grass there and discovered the outlines of two "missing" stones. This might mean that the stones were originally set in a circle, not a horseshoe shape. Over the past ten years, scientists have discovered new stones, burial pits, and even another "mini-Stonehenge" nearby.

The mystery of Stonehenge has led to all sorts of myths and folktales. At one time, some people believed that Merlin, the wizard from the tales of King Arthur, built the monument. One of the most famous rocks at Stonehenge lies outside the circle, so there's a legend that the devil dropped that stone there. But it's likely that modern people will never really understand the full truth about the site and what it meant to the ancient people of Britain.

Some neopagans come to Stonehenge to celebrate the Winter Solstice (the shortest day of the year) in December; as well as the spring and fall equinoxes (the midpoints between the summer and winter solstices) in March and September. The celebrations are much smaller than the one for the Summer Solstice, typically drawing 1,000 people or less. Wiccans aren't the only neopagans, but Wicca is by far the largest neopagan religion.

they come to Stonehenge, they don't cast evil spells or bring black cats.

The witches who visit Stonehenge all look different. Some wear flowers in their hair. Others carry wooden staffs. They can be women, and men, of all ages, shapes, colors, and sizes. They're not here to worship Satan. They don't cackle, or have green skin.

The ritual they perform is peaceful. First, the witches call on the North, South, East, and West. They chant the names of gods, goddesses, and other deities. Together, they celebrate the joy and fertility of the height of summer's glory. And they finish their sacred gathering with two words that have come to symbolize the modern-day witch: "Blessed be."

A NEW RELIGION

These witches don't hand out poisoned apples. In fact, most modern-day witches are normal people who just happen to believe in a neopagan religion called Wicca.

Instead of going to a church, synagogue, or regular meeting place, modern witches practice their religion alone, in small groups, and during occasional larger gatherings like the one at Stonehenge. Their beliefs and practices include elements of both modern ceremonies and ancient rituals. They find inspiration in the rhythms of nature, astronomy, and the seasons. And though many witches practice what they call "magick," this doesn't involve pulling rabbits out of hats or making things disappear.

So what makes them witches? How did witchcraft become a religion, anyway? What do modern witches believe? The answer is as long and rich as a magical spell. And it's been going on almost as long as humans have walked the Earth.

A History of Witches

The idea of magic, sorcery, and witchcraft has been around as long as humans have. But it took thousands of years before witches developed a bad reputation. In ancient times, witches were important and respected members of human society.

THE OLDEST WITCHES

More than 17,000 years ago, the earliest humans were still living in caves, agriculture had not yet been developed, and large creatures like woolly mammoths still roamed the Earth. And in the caves of Lascaux, France, prehistoric humans painted pictures of the oldest witches—mysterious magicians wearing buffalo heads.

Humans didn't have farms or live in cities yet, but they did live and work together in groups; use basic tools made from materials like wood, bone, or stone; control and use fire for cooking and warmth; and hunt for their food. They also made art inside their caves, some of which shows shamans (people we might call healers or medicine men today).

Did these medicine men help with the hunt? Did they communicate with the spirits of dead animals? What kind of magic did they practice? It's likely that we'll never know. More questions than answers lie deep in those ancient caves.

Modern experts believe that prehistoric cave paintings, such as this one made 30,000 years ago at Lascaux in France, were created by the shamans, or witch doctors, of Stone Age cultures. They may have represented a form of magic that would ensure a successful hunt, which was vital to the tribe's survival.

DEMONS AND SPIRITS

By around 3,200 BCE, the great civilizations of Mesopotamia and Egypt had formed, with each developing a written language. It is from their writings that we know the peoples of ancient Babylon and Egypt believed in magic and witches. People living in ancient Babylon believed that their lives were controlled by good and evil spirits they called demons.

Witches studied the ways of these demons in a practice called demonology. And since people thought that demons could live in a person's bed, seep into buildings through unsealed cracks, and haunt dreams, there was plenty to study.

Ancient Egypt had its share of demons, too—and Egyptians believed in the use of magic to help people live in harmony with mysterious gods and ghosts. Magicians called hekau chanted spells to protect humans from evil demons, or to curse enemies of the Pharaoh. Rich Egyptians who could afford to learn how to read collected healing spells, which were believed to help relieve sickness or to protect unborn children.

Even though this ancient magic involved spells, amulets, and interaction with the spirit world, it was a part of everyday life, rather than something weird or scary. People who were having trouble in their lives or wanted to hold on to a streak of good luck relied on witches to cast spells on their behalf. If the magic didn't work, that didn't mean it wasn't real; that meant some more powerful spell had prevented their magic from working properly.

High Magic, Low Magic

Ideas about the practice of magic evolved in the ancient civilizations of Greece, Rome, and Persia, from around 800 BCE to 600 CE. By the time the Greeks, Romans, and Persians built their huge empires, most people living in their cultures believed in magic and trusted that it could be used to affect their everyday lives. The use of magical herbs, wands, and spells became commonplace.

In ancient Egypt and Babylon, the word "demon" could mean either a good or a bad spirit.

Our modern English word magic derives from *Magi*, the name for a group of high magicians in the Persian civilization who functioned almost like priests. The Magi interpreted dreams, told fortunes, and even performed what we would consider magic tricks today. They also developed what we now think of as incantations—chants or spells meant to protect friends or curse enemies.

In the Greek, Roman, and Persian civilizations, there were two distinct levels of magic. Priests and religious or political leaders performed "high magic," or Theurgy. This involved important religious rituals for the benefit of the entire community, or for members of the

ALL ABOUT AMULETS

Ancient people loved their bling, but not for decoration. In fact, some of the most popular jewelry in the ancient world wasn't intended to be decorative jewelry at all. Often, necklaces and charms were worn as amulets—objects believed to offer protection against evil spirits, bad luck, or other dangers.

Here's how it worked: a person who wanted extra protection would get in touch with a witch or magician and ask them to provide an amulet to help them. People of all ages and classes wore amulets and they were incredibly popular. In ancient Egypt, dead people were buried with their amulets, in a belief that they could continue to help them in the afterlife!

Sometimes, amulets were inscribed with magic words meant to ward off sickness or scare away malicious demons. Other types of amulets were used to make requests. In the Greek and Roman world, "curse tablets" were carved or written with prayers for luck, complaints about other people, and hopes for success in battle. Then they were buried, dropped in a pool of water that was sacred to a god or goddess, left at a shrine, or otherwise hidden away in the hopes that the curse would come to pass.

Archaeologists have discovered all kinds of ancient amulets, from Egyptian scarabs to Roman gemstones associated with the different powers of the gods. People even use amulets today. Anyone who has ever seen someone wearing a crucifix necklace or carrying a four-leaf clover or rabbit's foot for good luck has seen an amulet!

ruling classes. They cast spells and called on the major deities of their culture to assist them in their work.

By contrast, witches worked with individuals, rather than the larger community. They performed Goetia, or "low magic," calling on minor spirits to help them resolve individual problems related to love, sickness, and everyday life.

Much of what we know about witches in the ancient world comes from myths and legends. One of the most famous witches in ancient Greek lore was Medea. She often cast spells to help her friends. In one story she created a magic potion that made her aged and infirm father-in-law young again. She could also use her magic to foretell the future.

Hecate was the Greek goddess of witchcraft. Ancient Greeks believed she could protect their homes. They built shrines to her near doorways in the hopes that her witchcraft would keep evil spirits out. The Romans believed in a similar goddess, which they called Trivia.

Mysterious Druids

The pagan religions of the Greeks, Romans, and Persians weren't the only ones in existence during ancient times. People living outside the sphere of these empires had their own beliefs, which also included magic and witchcraft. However, we don't know as much about the practices of these people, as they did not produce written accounts of what they did, how they practiced their religions, or even what they believed.

Thanks to Greek and Roman historians, soldiers, and travelers, modern scholars know a little bit about a mysterious group of pagan

A statue of Medea in Batumi Adjara, Georgia. A witch, and in some tales a priestess of Hectate, Medea is a notable figure in Greek mythology.

leaders who lived in the British Isles (England, Ireland, Scotland) as well as in northern Europe. They were called Druids. The Druids were responsible for the religion of the Celts, an ancient people who lived in these lands. They were in charge of the Celts' festivals, which revolved around a solar and lunar calendar. Romans who visited England in the first century reported that the Druids conducted human sacrifices.

Historians believe that the Druids were educated in astronomy and astrology. They were also believed to be able to practice magic. In general, the practices of the Druids were very similar to those of mod-

A MAGICIAN'S TOOLBOX

So what was in a magician's toolbox in ancient Greece? Archaeologists found out during the 1970s. During an excavation of the 4,000-year-old Greek city of Pergamon, in modern-day Turkey, they discovered a box that was probably owned by a magician.

The box was full of mysterious objects. Inside were a bronze table and dish covered with magical symbols, two bronze rings, a bronze nail with letters on it, and three stones inscribed with what might be the names of magical deities. Unfortunately, archaeologists aren't sure who this box belonged to, or how the items in it were actually used.

The ancient witch or magician who owned the kit would probably have used it to call on the gods, ask for good luck and healing, or bless objects so they could protect people from demons and bad luck. In contrast, a low magician's kit would have contained stones, herbs, and maybe a spell or two.

The Roman historian Pliny the Elder wrote that the Druids considered mistletoe to be a sacred plant. According to Pliny, the Druids used mistletoe berries to make healing potions, as well as in fertility rituals.

ern witches. They worshiped nature, and were supposed to be able to use their magic to predict the future. Druids used spells, magical rituals, and potions to practice their mysterious religion. However, unlike modern witches it's believed that only men could become Druids.

BECOMING WITCHES

Although the belief in magic was widespread during prehistoric and ancient times, not much is known about witches. This is probably because witches generally practiced "low magic," intended to help ordinary individuals with their everyday problems, so they were not considered important enough to write about.

Over time, the practices of low magicians were lumped into one category, known as "witchcraft." This word came to include all kinds of rituals that were pagan or non-Christian. For example, many people visited witches when they had health problems requiring medical treatment. By the Medieval age of western history (around 500 to 1500 CE), potions, the use of herbs, and things like amulets and chants were all thought of as witchcraft.

Among the people of Europe, there were plenty of stereotypes about witches. It was believed that they could shift shapes, cure diseases, and cast spells that could cause good (or bad) luck. And even as new beliefs about witches and witchcraft formed, old traditions kept on going.

BAD NEWS FOR WITCHES

During the first and second centuries of the common era (CE), the Christian religion began to spread throughout the Roman Empire. Over time, Christianity began to challenge and replace the pagan religions practiced by people in the empire. By the fifth century CE, Christianity was the official religion of Rome.

During the Medieval period, the Christian Church dominated most people's lives in Europe, the Middle East, and other former territories of the Roman Empire. Church leaders condemned those who practiced pagan religions, including witches. Ordinary people had once relied on witches and their low magic for medical advice and reassurance during hard times. However, as the Church gained control the old ways were outlawed and being labeled a "witch" became a bad thing.

Unfortunately, it was easy to call someone who was different a witch—even when she wasn't. Many of these so-called witches were probably people who passed on old folklore, used natural remedies to heal the sick, or simply continued to believe in the pagan gods and goddesses that their parents or grandparents had worshipped. However, as Christian leaders began to view witches as a threat, it wasn't long until witches were being accused of crimes and punished harshly.

Witches on Trial

Things began changing for the worse for witches toward the middle of the Medieval period. The Christian Church had survived the fall of the Roman Empire in 476 CE, and became the dominant religion of Europe. However, heretics—those who did not follow official Church teachings—often threatened the unity of the Church. To keep the Church together, Christian leaders took steps to stamp out all beliefs that were different. This included the pagan religions that people had practiced for centuries. Suddenly, witches were outlaws, and those who were accused of practicing witchcraft were placed on trial.

A Fever of Fear

At one time, the Christian Church simply ignored witches, teaching that there was no such thing as magic spells or witchcraft. However, over time the Church's position changed. Christian leaders taught that witches—who had long been associated with healing traditions and folk magic—were actually evil beings that did the work of Satan, the devil in the Jewish and Christian scriptures. Witches were blamed for many bad things that occurred, including wars, storms, and plagues.

Beginning in the 12th century, the Roman Catholic Church implemented a new program throughout Europe called the Inquisition. Its

This engraving by German artist Albrecht Dürer's, created around 1500, depicts a naked witch riding backward on a goat. Europeans experienced serious social upheaval during the Middle Ages due to the Protestant Reformation of the Christian church, as well as deadly plagues and wars fueled by religious differences. Witches became a convenient target for fearful communities.

purpose was to identify those who held beliefs that Church leaders thought posed a threat to their religious teachings. Those arrested by the Inquisition were often tortured until they agreed to give up their beliefs. Those punished by the Inquisition included witches, mostly women, who were suspected of devil worship or accused of practicing sorcery or black magic.

The Inquisition was only the beginning. By about the year 1400, fear of witches had become so widespread in Europe that many countries passed laws against witchcraft. With the introduction of these Witchcraft Acts, the legal punishment for being a witch was to burn at the stake. Suddenly, witch fever swept Europe. The period from 1450 through 1750 CE, during which more than 40,000 people were executed as witches in Europe and North America, has been nicknamed "the Great Witch Craze." Often, witches were accused of making secret deals with Satan, who gave them their magic powers. Witches were accused of flying on broomsticks, ruining crops, and even killing babies in the womb.

HUNTING WITCHES

People of Medieval Europe believed they had many reasons to fear witches. They also had new ways to share their fears with others. The newly invented printing press, along with better roads and methods of

This painting by the 19th century Spanish artist Eugenio Lucas Velázquez shows a woman condemned of witchcraft by the Inquisition. Accused witches were often publicly ridiculed on they way to their execution.

A WITCH-HUNTER'S HANDBOOK

How did witch hunters identify a witch? They turned to an unusual best-selling book published in the late 1400s: *Malleus Maleficarum* (Latin for "The Hammer of Witches"). This book told would-be witch hunters how to recognize, prosecute, and torture witches. It became more and more popular as the Great Witch Craze reached its peak, and is the source of many modern stereotypes about witches.

The author of *Malleus Maleficarum* was a Roman Catholic priest, Heinrich Kramer, who had tried to find and punish witches in the Tyrol mountains of central Europe during the 1480s. The Catholic bishop of the region thought Kramer was crazy, and sent the priest away. Kramer used his book to write about his belief in witchcraft, as well as his ideas about the things witches did, and the reasons that they did them. It frightened many people—who wouldn't be scared by accounts of witches stealing babies to use their ground-up bones in potions, flying through the air, and even sacrificing and eating humans?

Though the book's claims were wild and dramatic, many people took it seriously—so seriously that they began to drown, hang, and even burn people they accused of witchcraft. Even though the Catholic Church officially said that the book was false, dozens of editions were published over the next three centuries.

Malleus Maleficarum convinced many people that women were particularly susceptible to becoming witches. After its publication, more and more women were accused of being witches. At its peak, three quarters of all people accused of witchcraft were women.

This mural from a Christian monastery in Bulgaria depicts bat-winged demons influencing a woman who practiced witchcraft (top right panel) as well as those practicing folk magic (bottom panel). As leaders of the Medieval Christian church began trying to stamp out heretical beliefs, they promoted the idea that witches were to blame for failed crops, dead babies, and sickness in their communities.

transportation, made it easier than ever before to spread news and information. This caused fear to spread more quickly as well.

As the fear of witches intensified, citizens began to take matters into their own hands. They banded together for "witch hunts." They would find witches, and hand them over officials for trial and punishment.

Some people used the fear of witches as a way to take revenge on families or individuals they didn't like. Sometimes, those who were accused of witchcraft were wealthy people who challenged Church

Witch hunters looked for a "devil's mark" when examining witches. They usually found what they were looking for—any mole, birthmark, or skin tag would do. A woman accused of witchcraft was often poked with a pin during her trial, to see if any insensitive portion of her body could be found. If the spot did not bleed when pricked, it was a devil's mark.

power or the authority of local government officials. Other times, they were poor women who had offended a priest or angered a neighbor. Sometimes, older women were accused of witchcraft because they were suffering from a disease like dementia. Other times, the accusation was made to get a person out of the way so that another relative could inherit a family's wealth.

Innocent people were often accused, tried, and executed as witches. The witch hunts continued even when it was proven that the people being arrested were harmless. Even worse, some people who were accused of witchcraft made false confessions in hopes they would be treated with mercy. Their attempts to avoid harm only increased concern about witches, and more people joined in the madness. Major witch hunts and trials occurred in the central European cities of Trier (from 1581 to 1593), Fulda (from 1603 to 1606), Würzburg (from

1626 to 1631), and Bamberg (also from 1626 to 1631). Other notable trials were held in North Berwick, Scotland, during the 1590s; at Lancashire, England, in 1612; and at Torsåker, Sweden, in 1675, when 71 people were executed.

Today, historians view the witch hunts of this period as a form of mass hysteria, in which a large group of people become suspicious of something they perceive to be a threat, then act together to eradicate it. At the time, even highly educated people were superstitious and terrified of the devil. Instead of accepting that tragic events like terrible snowstorms, scary diseases, or unexplained deaths are part of life, people pointed the finger at the people they called witches—even when those people were young women or even children.

WITCH TRIALS AT SALEM

One of the best-known witch hunts took place in Salem, Massachusetts, during the 1690s. It started with a group of young girls who began to have "fits," or seizures. At first, three women were arrested and accused of causing the fits through their witchcraft. One was a homeless woman. Another was a woman who rarely attended church. A third was an African American, or possibly Native American, servant. All were different from the norm of the community, and were therefore easy targets for the accusation of witchcraft.

However, soon other women, and even some men, were accused of witchcraft in the Salem community. Many of them were respectable, churchgoing people. People came out in droves to see these accused "witches" on trial. Anyone who defended them risked being labeled a witch themselves. Historians now believe that a dispute between two families may have driven some of the accusations.

Once a person was accused of witchcraft in Massachusetts, she or he was jailed and subjected to horrible trials. Accused persons were encouraged to confess, even if they were innocent. A person who didn't confess was subjected to scary and often ridiculous tests to determine whether she or he was a witch. Some accused witches were asked to recite the Lord's Prayer or read from the Bible without stuttering, mumbling, or missing a word. This test is harder than it seems,

The historic home of Judge Jonathan Corwin in Salem, Massachusetts, is now known as the "Witch House." It is the only standing structure with ties to the Salem Witchcraft Trials of 1692.

as accused witches were often uneducated, and were so frightened that they could not help but slip up.

Another test was the "ordeal by water." It involved tying weights to a suspected witch and dropping her into a deep river or lake. If the woman floated, she was considered a witch and was subject to execution. If she sank, it showed that she was innocent. Of course, the women who sank almost always drowned—but at least they had proven that they weren't witches!

"Pressing," in which heavy stones were placed on the accused person's chest, was another test. The weight of the stones was supposed to make the accused witch confess; however, if he or she did not admit guilt, more weight was added until the person could no longer talk or breathe, and was crushed to death. An 80-year-old farmer named Giles Corey, who was accused of being a warlock (a male witch), was killed this way at Salem in September 1692. His wife Martha was hanged as a witch three days afterward.

In addition to the Coreys, 18 other people—most of them women—were executed for witchcraft at Salem between February 1692 and the end of the trials in May 1693. Nearly 200 others were in prison, awaiting their fate, when colonial authorities intervened and ordered them to be released. In the decades that followed, the people who were arrested during the Salem Witch Trials were shown to have been innocent. Today, they are remembered as victims of a bizarre episode of American history.

THE WITCH CRAZE DIES DOWN

During the early 18th century, the mass hysteria over witchcraft died down in Europe and North America. As society changed, educated people began to reject superstitious beliefs in spirits and magic.

Historians now think that the "fits" suffered by girls in Salem were caused by mass hysteria, a collective delusion about a threat to society that spreads rapidly through rumors and fear. Another possible cause is poisoning by ergot, a fungus that occurs naturally in the grains that members of the Massachusetts Bay colony used to make bread. The symptoms of ergot poisoning include hallucinations and convulsions.

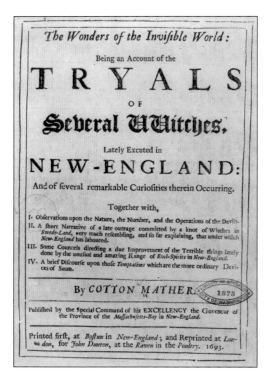

Cotton Mather, a well-known religious leader in the Massachusetts colony, wrote about the Salem Witch Trials in 1693.

Governments stopped encouraging witch hunts, and in fact passed laws to eliminate them. For example, in 1735 the British parliament passed the Witchcraft Act. According to this law, there was no such thing as witchcraft, and someone who accused another person of being a witch could be punished by up to a year in jail. This law ended witch hunts in Great Britain, as well as in its American colonies.

However, despite the end of the Great Witch Craze, people who believed in folk magic, herbalism, and the healing arts continued to be secretive about such practices. The Witchcraft Act of 1735 also made it illegal for anyone to claim that they could communicate with spirits or perform healing magic.

For the next two centuries, it seemed like witchcraft might be gone for good. But during the 20th century, the practice of witchcraft would make a return to the public consciousness.

In 1878, nearly 200 years after the Salem Witch Trials, a Massachusetts woman filed a lawsuit in a Salem court accusing a man named Daniel Spofford of ruining her health by practicing "mesmerism," and influencing her mind and body with evil intent. However, the case was dismissed. Most people consider this the last witch trial in the United States.

WITCHCRAFT ON THE RISE

After centuries of witch hunts, persecution, and execution, it seemed like witchcraft was finished for good by the early 20th century. If there were any witches left, they would have to practice their magic in secret. But that all changed in a small cottage in England during the 1940s when the witches came back—and a new religion was born.

WITCHES COME BACK

In 1939, a man named Gerald Gardner went to visit a few of his friends in the town of Highcliffe, England. What happened next was extraordinary. According to Gardner, his friends took him to visit a wealthy woman who lived nearby. He entered her home a normal person, but he left a witch.

We will never know what exactly took place during the secret initiation ritual Gardner and his friends participated in, but a few details are clear from his writings. He was stripped naked. He listened to chants and incantations. And at some point during that evening, he heard the word "wica" (an Old English word meaning "witch") for the first time.

Later in life, Gardner would make many claims about the witches who initiated him that evening. Inside that house, he realized that witchcraft was not dead after all. And he wanted to tell the world.

Gerald Gardner wrote several books about witchcraft: High Magic's Aid *(1949),* Witchcraft Today *(1954), and* The Meaning of Witchcraft *(1959). The form of Wicca based on his writings and teachings is known as Gardnerian Wicca. Over time, some of Gardner's followers left to start their own Wicca traditions.*

INSIDE THE COTTAGE

The witches who initiated Gardner were known as the New Forest coven. (A coven is a word used to describe a gathering of witches.) Many were friends of Gardner, who had always been fascinated by mediums, spirituality, and the occult. Though Gardner later claimed that the coven had links to ancient groups of witches, its members probably had been meeting for less than a decade when he joined.

Gardner was thrilled. He bought a small, primitive cottage in the countryside that, it was rumored, had been owned by a witch during the 16th century. He let the coven use this cottage. There, they performed rituals, danced in a circle, and cast spells. To develop their rituals, the witches drew on information they found in old textbooks of magic, known as grimoires.

The members of the New Forest coven did not intend to create a new religion. But Gardner was not content to let their rituals remain hidden in his cottage. As an anthropologist and student of English folklore, he wanted to tell the world about the spells and rites of these modern-day witches. During the late 1940s and 1950s, he wrote books and articles about the activities and beliefs of his coven, which he eventually renamed the Bricket Wood coven. Others who were interested in supernatural phenomena and the occult became attracted to this new practice, which became known as Wicca.

WICCA IS BORN

Gardner was controversial, but today he is known as the Father of Wicca. He published books, met other witches, and even founded a museum of witchcraft. His enthusiasm was contagious. He believed so strongly that he was helping to bring back an ancient religion that others couldn't help but believe. People who were tired of established religions like Christianity, and were searching for new things to believe in, discovered and investigated Wicca.

Although Gardner spread the word about Wicca, the religion developed without a hierarchy of leaders. Practices differed from coven to coven. Wiccans claimed that they practiced white magic, not

Gardner used this restored 16th century cottage near the village of Bricket Wood to hold meetings of the early Wicca community. The group that met there eventually became known as the Bricket Wood coven.

THE BOOK OF SHADOWS

How do witches learn spells and rituals? Some consult a "Book of Shadows," which contains different spells, rites, and texts. In fact, many covens and witches keep their own Book of Shadows—but each looks a bit different from the rest.

The first Book of Shadows was probably created by Gerald Gardner, the father of modern Wicca. Though Gardner claimed that it was an ancient tradition, it is likely that he invented it during the 1940s. Gardner's Book of Shadows was kind of like a cookbook for witches. Individuals or members of a coven could use it to record and pass down spells, beliefs, and rituals. They could add new ones, or take out things that they felt were outdated or didn't work.

Today, many witches and covens keep their own Book of Shadows. Each book looks different and contains different information. Sometimes a coven has a master book, from which members copy down the spells they choose to know. Other times, Wiccan teachers pass the books along to their students. The books can be handwritten, or even kept online. Some people believe that a witch's Book of Shadows should be burned after his or her death, but others think they should be passed down from generation to generation.

Not everyone subscribes to the idea of a Book of Shadows. In fact, some witches think that spells shouldn't be written down at all. They prefer to pass on their rituals to others using oral traditions.

evil black magic, and their religion evolved to embrace many ways of celebrating the year and different rites of passage.

Even though Wicca incorporated some ancient ideas and practices, it also had modern appeal. Instead of excluding people who didn't believe the "right" things, Wiccans included all kinds of people. Instead of worshiping religious figures in churches, Wiccans focused on the wisdom of the Earth and could be practiced by anyone, anywhere. Soon, Wicca spread from England to Europe, the United States, Canada, and other countries around the world.

A NEW AGE

Neopagan religions such as Wicca are sometimes known as "New Age" religions. This term refers to religions that combine many traditions and call on both old and new ideas. Most New Age religions are inclusive and invite diverse viewpoints and participants. Neopaganism and Wicca often go hand in hand with other New Age practices like crystal healing, astrology, meditation, and alternative medicine.

As more people began to identify as Wiccan, a debate broke out. Is Wicca really a religion? Since Wicca has no priests or sacred scriptures that contain rules that everyone must obey, it can be hard to tell. Unlike most religions, Wicca is largely based on an individual's per-

Those who hold neo-pagan worldviews, such as Wiccans, believe that the natural world contains many deities and spirits, and that humans can communicate with these spirits and draw on their power through their rituals.

An initiation is the first step to becoming a witch, and can be performed alone or as part of a coven.

sonal experiences. Every Wiccan decides for himself or herself how to interpret and practice the religion.

Gerald Gardner claimed that Wicca is linked to an ancient witch-religion that existed before recorded language. However, most Wiccan traditions actually originated in the 1940s. In addition, Wicca does draw some rituals and beliefs from well-established world religions.

When the first generation of Wiccans began to have children and raise them in Wiccan traditions, the question of whether Wicca was really a religion became more important. These parents wanted their children to have the same rights and religious freedoms as those who followed mainstream religions like Christianity or Judaism. Some Wiccans found themselves seeking legal recognition of a religion that others didn't recognize as legitimate.

Although originally Wiccan covens had each held separate and original beliefs and practices, during the 1970s some Wiccans decided to organize in order to gain legal protection. In the United States, groups like the Covenant of the Goddess began managing covens and setting out ground rules for the practice of Wicca. Their efforts worked. In 1986, the U.S. government officially recognized Wicca as a religion. Since the 1990s, in many states Wiccan covens have successfully received a religious exemption from paying taxes. In 2007, the U.S. military agreed to allow Wiccan symbols such as the pentacle (a five-pointed star) on the gravestones of deceased soldiers.

In The Broom Closet

Despite wider recognition of Wicca, some Wiccans still face discrimination and intolerance. Many people incorrectly confuse Wicca with Satanism, or worship of the devil described in the Jewish and Christian scriptures. The military does not permit pagan chaplains, and prisons often deny incarcerated Wiccans access to the herbs and oils they need to perform rituals.

Because of this, some Wiccans choose to keep their beliefs "in the broom closet," or hidden from others. They may keep their practices entirely secret, or avoid using the word "witch" to refer to their activities. Thus Wicca remains a solitary craft for many people. However, thanks to the Internet, over the past two decades it has become easier for those interested in Wicca to learn about the religion and its practices.

A RITUAL FOR SPRING EQUINO

Flowers should be lai
around the circle and
The cau
and
w   ll.
on the altar.

range the
and cast
Recite the   ll.

wh

nd

O great
p
the
rips

UNDERSTANDING WICCA

nlike most organized religions, such as Christianity, Judaism, or Islam, Wicca is a religion without authoritative leaders or strict rules. There are no sacred scriptures, and no required gathering places. Wiccans believe different things and practice in different ways. Despite this, Wicca has become one of the world's fastest-growing religions. It is rich in both ancient and modern traditions.

THE WICCAN REDE

"An' it harm none, do what ye will." This sentence, known as the Wiccan Rede, is the closest Wiccans come to a universal tenet or belief. The word rede is an ancient word that means "advice." The rede tells Wiccans that they can do what they want, as long as their actions don't harm others.

One of the reasons the rede is so popular with Wiccans is that it's open to interpretation. It is framed as advice or counsel instead of as a strict commandment, so people can choose to follow it or not. And nobody can say what "harm none" really means, or what the consequences would be for violating this advice. Every Wiccan must interpret the rede for herself or himself.

Some people compare the Wiccan Rede to the idea of karma (what goes around comes around) or to the Golden Rule (do unto others as you would have them do unto you) of the Judeo-Christian tradition. However, because the rede is open to interpretation, it's much like Wicca itself, in which each coven determines its own practices and worship rituals.

WHAT WICCANS WORSHIP

Even though Wicca is known for not having a single belief or world-view, most people agree that the religion is pagan and nature-based. Many Wiccans worship both a male god and a female goddess. They believe these two deities are like two sides of the same coin, with energies that complement and balance one another.

Wiccans call their masculine deity the Horned God. This figure is associated with the hunt, nature, wild animals (including humans), and the sun. The feminine deity is called the Mother Goddess, or sometimes the Triple Goddess. This goddess is seen as having three

THE THIRTEEN PRINCIPLES

In 1974, a group of Wiccans called The Council of American Witches created a statement called "The Principles of Wiccan Belief." This document lays out the practices of many Wiccans and neopagans, from nature worship to an intriguing definition of "witch."

> Calling oneself "Witch" does not make a Witch—but neither does heredity itself, nor the collecting of titles, degrees, and initiations. A Witch seeks to control the forces within her/him that make life possible in order to live wisely and well without harm to others and in harmony with Nature.

To this day, many Wiccans use "The Thirteen Principles," as they are called, as a statement of their beliefs. But that doesn't mean that each and every Wiccan believes the same thing or worships in the same way. The Thirteen Principles are just a guideline.

The complete text of the Thirteen Principles can be found in the appendix to this book on pages 54-55.

In Wicca, the male deity is associated with nature, hunting, and the sun. In the United Kingdom, the male deity of Wicca is often depicted as the Green Man, a treelike figure that is venerated in springtime fertility rituals.

elements: young woman, mother, and old crone. The goddess is associated with unity, fertility, and the moon.

Some Wiccans only worship the Mother Goddess. Others worship many other deities and spirits in addition to the Horned God and Mother Goddess. They pay tribute to pagan deities from Norse, Greek, Roman, Egyptian, and Celtic traditions.

Nature and the seasons are extremely important in most Wicca traditions. The traditional Wiccan festivals revolve around the changes in nature as the year progresses. Nature is often seen as a deity itself, and worshiped accordingly. Some Wiccans believe that a spirit called "the One" lives everywhere in nature.

HOW WICCANS WORSHIP

Wiccans can practice their religion alone, and do not have to worship with others. However, many Wiccans join a group called a coven. Usually, covens have their own rules and traditions that include how many people can join (some covens are capped at 13 members), who leads the group (sometimes a coven will have a High Priestess or High Priest), when they meet, and what the members do.

Many covens accept new initiates with a ceremony, and then lead them through a period of study known as an "apprenticeship," which

Some witches perform their rituals "skyclad," or without wearing any clothes. This is because certain covens believe when clothing is removed, social status is also, making their rituals purer and more equal. However, not all witches agree with this, and no one is ever required to take off their clothes to be a Wiccan.

usually lasts for a year and one day. During an apprenticeship, a student learns history, studies the coven's traditions, and learns all about the use of magic (sometimes called "the Craft"). Apprentices are usually forbidden to take part in rituals or cast spells.

Once an apprenticeship is through, the apprentice dedicates himself or herself to Wicca and begins to practice the religion, including spells and rituals. Many covens meet at every full moon to work magic together. Together, they celebrate sabbats (holidays) and esbats (full moons).

A ritual called "Drawing Down the Moon" is one of the most powerful and important Wiccan ceremonies. In this ritual, a Wiccan priestess calls upon the Mother Goddess. Wiccans believe the priestess goes into a trance, in which the Goddess enters the priestess's body and speaks to the coven through her. Since the person who leads the "drawing down" ritual is possessed by the goddess, Wiccans see the ritual as particularly sacred. (A similar, though more rarely performed ritual, is "Drawing Down the Sun," in which a male priest's body is occupied by the spirit of the Horned God.) These "drawing down" rituals provide a way for Wiccans to interact directly with their deities.

WHEN WICCANS WORSHIP

Wiccans think of the year as a circle—the "wheel of the year"—instead of as a straight line. This circle represents the typical life cycle of death and rebirth, and includes all of the festivals and celebrations important to Wiccans. The circle includes eight "sabbat" celebrations, each with its own customs and traditions. Sabbats that fall on solstices or equinox-

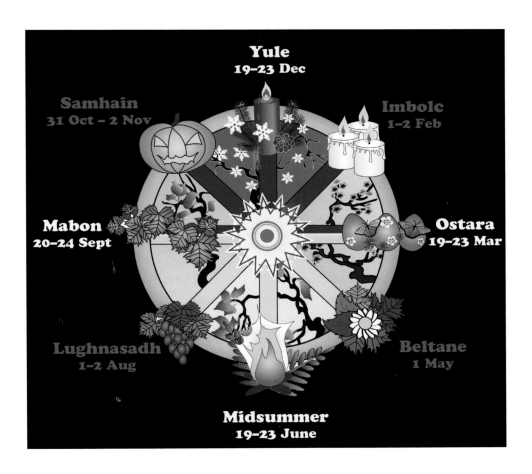

es are known as "quarter days." Festivals held on the midpoints between the solstices and equinoxes are known as "cross quarter days."

Like other aspects of Wicca, there are many different ways to celebrate a Wiccan holiday. Some people celebrate by themselves. Others join a coven or another group to observe the following holidays:

YULE (WINTER SOLSTICE): This celebration takes place during mid-winter and foreshadows the first movements of life after winter.

IMBOLC: It's time to celebrate spring—this celebration focuses on cleaning and purification as the year begins.

OSTARA (VERNAL EQUINOX): The spring equinox is celebrated with flowers and rituals marking equal light and darkness.

BELTANE: This early summer celebration is all about fertility and feasts. Sometimes a maypole is used. Many weddings take place at Beltane.

MIDSUMMER (SUMMER SOLSTICE): This is the longest day of the year, and dark nights will soon overtake long days. This celebration, also known as Litha, includes flames and tributes to the Horned God.

LUGHNASADH: Also called Lammas, this is the first of three festivals celebrating the harvest.

MABON (AUTUMNAL EQUINOX): Light and darkness are equal again, and the fall harvest is celebrated with music and drinking.

SAMHAIN: This holiday coincides with Halloween, and is a time for Wiccans to remember the dead.

Because sabbats depend on the relationship of the Earth to the Sun, the dates of these festivals can vary depending on where in the world the sabbat will be celebrated. For example, Wiccans living in countries in the Northern Hemisphere, such as the United States, Britain, or Europe, celebrate the Winter Solstice around December 21 or 22. However, Wiccans living in the Southern Hemisphere (for example, in South America or Australia) would celebrate the Winter Solstice between June 20 and June 22.

When covens or groups of Wiccans meet outside of sabbats, the meetings are known as "esbats." The word esbat comes from an ancient French word that means "frolic," and esbats are usually

A celebration of Beltane in Edinburgh, Scotland. Beltane, an ancient Celtic festival, is observed on May 1.

intended to be celebrations. Often, esbats are held when there is a full moon, as this is associated with the female energy of the Mother Goddess.

MAGIC

Magic, or Craft, is what connects Wicca to the witches of legend. When Wiccans talk about magic, they're not referring to pulling a rabbit out of a hat or making something disappear. In fact, that's why some Wiccans refer to their power as magick, not magic—this alternative spelling is meant to differentiate their power from the sleight-of-hand tricks used by stage magicians.

Wiccans believe that the natural world is bound together by a powerful energy force, which is unseen yet connected to all living things.

They believe that if they are in proper balance with that force, they have the power to make changes in their lives, as well as in the lives of others. A Wiccan can draw on this power by performing rituals or casting spells.

Most witches begin their rituals by "casting a circle." They use a wand or dagger to draw an imaginary circle of sacred energy. This sacred circle is a place in which positive energy and power are focused, and it prevents negative energy from entering to disturb the ritual. Generally, candles or markers are set at the circle's boundaries to indicate north, east, south, and west, and there is an altar in the center with all the tools needed for the ritual. The Wiccans who are participating enter the area from the east before casting the circle around themselves.

Not all Wiccans cast spells or attempt to use magic. Those who do, however, generally use many different types of spells. Some are passed from generation to generation; others are developed alone. Spells are a sort of magic language that is intended to draw on the positive energy of nature to create change. Spells can bless a person, or sanctify an event. They can be cast to gain health, wealth, or knowledge, or for protection, or even to help let go of a bad memory. Spells can be cast by individuals, or by groups.

THE THREEFOLD LAW

Some witches will say, "Mind the Threefold Law ye should, three times bad and three times good." The Threefold Law, or Rule of Three, holds that the energy—positive or negative—that a person puts out into the world will be returned three times over.

Since Wiccans believe in personal responsibility, they often ask themselves how their actions will affect others. If a witch believes in the Threefold Law, she knows that hating someone means her hate will come back threefold. Loving someone will bring back three times as much love. She'll think twice before acting—after all, her actions will be multiplied by three!

Witches call on five elements in their rituals: Earth, Water, Air, Fire, and Aether. While many spells are passed down from teacher to student, witches can also write their own spells.

While casting a spell, a witch will envision the desired outcome and try use her mind to direct the force of nature toward that end. The words of the spell only provide part of its power. The witch's tone of voice, the setting in which it is cast, and the tools used in the ritual are also important.

TOOLS AND SYMBOLS

Someone who practices the Craft can turn almost anything into a tool. However, Wiccans mostly rely on four primary tools: the wand, the dagger, the chalice, and the paten disk.

The wand should be familiar to anyone who has seen a witch on television or in a movie. Many witches make their own wands out of tree branches, although some wands are made from crystal or metal. The wand is associated with the element air. Wiccans believe their wands can direct and move natural energies.

The dagger can be any sort of blade. Usually, though, it is a ceremonial double-bladed knife with a black handle called an athame. The athame is associated with the element of fire. Athames are never meant to be used to cut or harm someone. The athame is often used to start spells by casting a circle.

The chalice is a goblet, or cup. It can be made of nearly any material: wood, brass, silver, or even stone. The chalice is associated with the

A pentagram is a five-point-ed star inscribed within a circle. Some people believe that when two points of the star point upward, as in the example pictured here, it represents a symbol of evil.

element of water and is used to hold liquids that are needed for rituals.

The paten disk is a tool used to consecrate an altar before a ritual. It is a round metal plate, often covered in symbols such as the pentacle, a five-pointed star within a circle. The pentacle is associated with the element of earth. Sometimes Wiccans carry protective amulets that bear this symbol; these are also called pentacles. Other symbols used by Wiccans include runes (ancient Norse letters) and hieroglyphic symbols used by ancient Egyptians. These symbols might be inscribed on jewelry, written in a Book of Shadows, or carved into a ritual space.

SO MOTE IT BE

At the end of spells, chants, prayers, and readings, Wiccans often say, "so mote it be." The phrase, which originated in Masonic writings of the 15th century, uses the ancient Saxon word mote, or "must." So in modern English the phrase means, "so it must be" or "so may it be." It's a way of ending or sealing a ritual or spell, sort of like the word "Amen" at the end of a Christian prayer.

MODERN-DAY WITCHES

People who spend time with a modern witch might hear him or her utter a simple phrase: "Blessed be." The words are the equivalent of the Indian word Namaste or the Hawaiian aloha, in that they are used as a greeting or goodbye. When someone says, "Blessed be," they are wishing the other person well. Some people believe that this practice makes Wicca a particularly welcoming religion.

Since Wicca doesn't have the institutions and organizations we associate with other religions, it can be hard to count witches, let alone track their activities. In 2000, a group of Wiccans called the Covenant of the Goddess conducted a poll of over 32,000 Wiccans in the United States. Here's what they found:

- About 71 percent of Wiccans are female witches. 29 percent are male witches.
- There are more young witches than older ones—in the poll, only 1 percent were 60 or older and 65 percent were between the ages of 18 and 39.
- There are self-identified witches and pagans in every state in the United States.
- The states with the highest number of witches were California and Texas.

WITCHES IN POPULAR CULTURE

While Wicca has become more accepted in modern culture, that doesn't mean old stereotypes of witchcraft are dead. There are still plenty of old-fashioned witches depicted on television shows, movies, and in popular culture. The out-of-date ideas about witchcraft are so powerful that they probably won't die out any time soon.

In most older movies and television shows, witches are shown using black magic for evil purposes. These witches often wear long robes and pointy black hats. Their skin might be green, or covered in hideous moles. They have black cats, stir their potions in huge cauldrons, cast spells with their wands, and fly around on brooms. Elphaba, the Wicked Witch of the West from *The Wizard of Oz*, is probably the best-known example of this witch stereotype. Another is Maleficent, the villain from the 1959 Disney film *Sleeping Beauty*.

More recently, television shows like *Sabrina the Teenage Witch* and *Wizards of Waverly Place* portrayed young adults as witches who are powerful, mysterious, and even funny. These witches use their powers to resolve problems in their everyday lives. The Harry Potter series of books and films feature witches who work for good, such as Hermione Granger and Minerva McGonagall, as well as evil witches like Bellatrix Lestrange. C.S. Lewis's book *The Lion, The Witch, and the Wardrobe*, which was made into a film in 2005, features an evil White Witch who imposes an eternal winter upon the land of Narnia.

There are very few popular movies or television shows that portray actual, practicing witches. The 1996 film *The Craft* and the 1998 movie *Practical Magic* each included some references to traditional Wicca practices. However, these films also drew on the old Hollywood stereotypes of witches and witchcraft to entertain viewers.

In 2008, the U.S. Census Bureau reported that 342,000 adults identified as Wiccan in the United States. Today, the Census Bureau estimates that, including children, there are more than 408,000 Americans who practice Wicca. This would make it the seventh-largest religious classification in the United States, after Christianity (226 million), Judaism (6.8 million), Islam (3.7 million), Buddhism (2.8 million), Hinduism (1.2 million), and Unitarian Universalism (930,000).

LIFE AS A MODERN-DAY WITCH

Most modern-day witches live normal, unassuming lives. They work, go to school, raise families, watch movies, play games online. They serve in the military and play sports. It's tempting to want to lump Wiccans into one category, but there is no typical witch.

It can be difficult to identify a modern witch just by clothing or hair. Some Wiccans wear pentacle symbols as jewelry. But others don't wear any kind of identification at all. Modern-day witches look just like anyone else. It's also hard to identify Wiccans by how they learn their craft. Not all witches belong to covens, and not all witches who belong to covens go through an apprenticeship year.

The Internet has dramatically changed the way modern witches worship. Some Wiccans used to feel isolated or ostracized. Today, they

Brooms are sometimes used by Wiccans, but not for transportation. Instead, a witch may use a broom called a besom to symbolically sweep a space clean before casting a spell.

The phrase "Blessed be" comes from a Wiccan ritual known as the Five Fold Kiss, in which various parts of the body are kissed to acknowledge the sacred qualities within. As each body part is kissed, a blessing that begins with the words "blessed be" is recited.

can find other like-minded people with the click of a mouse. In fact, many witches initially learn about witchcraft by reading and searching online.

MAKING MAGIC WORK

People think of magic as a special, or unusual, thing. But Wiccans who practice the Craft work to make magic part of their everyday lives. They do this through ritual, meditation, and their efforts to live in harmony with the seasons and the natural cycles of the sun and moon.

Unlike the witches shown in television shows and movies, modern-day witches can't shoot fire from their hands or transform people into frogs. Instead, modern witches find other ways to use their beliefs to drive change in the world. One poll found that roughly 86 percent of self-identified Wiccans and Pagans are registered to vote. This indicates that witches don't just sit back and wait for their magic to happen. Instead, they actively participate in politics to effect social changes.

The environment is a special cause for many Wiccans. After all, they worship the Earth's rhythms and try to learn nature's secrets. In August 2014, the Covenant of the Goddess, which represents a large group of Wiccans, made its first official statement about nature and the environment. "We commit to support efforts to rebalance our wondrous world for future generations," the statement said. "We know that climate change presents an imminent threat to humanity and other life on Earth. Since this imbalance is caused by human activity, we humans must accept responsibility for our actions and seek to reverse the damage and restore the balance. We support local, regional, national, and global efforts to conserve natural resources, to seek clean, sustainable sources of energy, and to rebalance our world." The organization currently works with other groups that try to conserve natural resources and oppose climate change.

Some witches work to change the world. Others work to spread their religion. They form small covens, reading and study groups, and join larger organizations. They fight stereotypes of witches and try to educate others.

THE FUTURE OF WICCA

A belief in magic and witchcraft has existed since the early days of human civilization. Some of the traditions practiced by Wiccans today are similar to rituals conducted long before the ancients built Stonehenge. But even though almost every aspect of Wicca is open to debate and up to individual interpretation, most witches welcome the future as much as the past.

As the 11th of the 13 Principles says, "As American witches, we are not threatened by debates on the history of the Craft, the origins of various terms, the origins of various aspects of different traditions. We are concerned with our present and our future."

Sure, witches have wands. They cast spells. They believe in magic and mystery. But many Wiccans would say that being brave enough to accept the past and look forward to the future is the most magical practice of all.

According to the United Nations, thousands of women worldwide are the victims of "witch hunts" each year. Most of these occur in developing countries, where superstition about black magic is widespread, such as in Africa or places like Fiji and Papua New Guinea.

Appendix

The Principles of Wiccan Belief

Editor's note: during the early 1970s, a group of modern-day witches met in Minneapolis. Calling themselves the Council of American Witches, in April 1974 the organization issued the following text, titled "The Principles of Wiccan Belief," or the Thirteen Principles. Although the Council of American Witches disbanded soon after, many American Wiccans continue to endorse and observe most or all of the Thirteen Principles.

1. We practice rites to attune ourselves with the natural rhythm of life forces marked by the phases of the Moon and the seasonal Quarters and Cross Quarters.
2. We recognize that our intelligence gives us a unique responsibility towards our environment. We seek to live in harmony with Nature, in ecological balance offering fulfillment to life and consciousness within an evolutionary concept.
3. We acknowledge a depth of power far greater than that is apparent to the average person. Because it is far greater than ordinary it is sometimes called "supernatural," but we see it as lying within that which is naturally potential to all.
4. We conceive of the Creative Power in the universe as manifesting through polarity—as masculine and feminine—and that this same Creative Power lies in all people, and functions through the interaction of the masculine and feminine. We value neither above the other, knowing each to be supportive of the other. We value sex as pleasure, as the symbol and embodiment of life, and as one of the sources of energies used in magickal practice and religious worship.

5. We recognize both outer and inner, or psychological, worlds—sometimes known as the Spiritual World, the Collective Unconscious, Inner Planes, etc.—and we see in the interaction of these two dimensions the basis for paranormal phenomena and magickal exercises. We neglect neither dimension for the other, seeing both as necessary for our fulfillment.

6. We do not recognize any authoritarian hierarchy, but do honor those who teach, respect those who share their greater knowledge and wisdom, and acknowledge those who have courageously given of themselves in leadership.

7. We see religion, magick and wisdom-in-living as being united in the way one views the world and lives within it—a world-view and philosophy of life which we identify as Witchcraft, the Wiccan Way.

8. Calling oneself "witch" does not make one a Witch—but neither does heredity itself, nor the collecting of titles, degrees, and initiations. A Witch seeks to control the forces within her/himself that make life possible in order to live wisely and well without harm to others and in harmony with Nature.

9. We believe in the affirmation and fulfillment of life in a continuation of evolution and development of consciousness, that gives meaning to the Universe we know, and our personal role within it.

10. Our only animosity towards Christianity, or toward any other religion or philosophy of life, is to the extent that its institutions have claimed to be "the only way," and have sought to deny freedom to others and to suppress other ways of religious practice and belief.

11. As American Witches, we are not threatened by debates on the history of the Craft, the origins of various terms, or the origins of various aspects of different traditions. We are concerned with our present and our future.

12. We do not accept the concept of absolute evil, nor do we worship any entity known as "Satan" or "the Devil", as defined by Christian tradition. We do not seek power through the suffering of others, nor do we accept that personal benefit can be derived only by denial to another.

13. We believe that we should seek within Nature that which is contributory to our health and well-being.

CHRONOLOGY

15000 BCE	Prehistoric people draw a medicine man on the walls of a cave in Lascaux, France.
3150 BCE	Ancient Egyptians use amulets to protect themselves.
1894 BCE	Ancient Babylonians study demons and spirits.
c. 400 BCE	Modern magic takes root in ancient Greece and Rome
c. 77 CE	Pliny the Elder's *Naturalis Historia* refers to a Druidic fertility ritual that uses mistletoe berries and involves the sacrifice of a white bull.
c. 100	The Christian book *Acts of the Apostles* describes an encounter between the Apostle Peter and a powerful magician named Simon Magus.
380	Christianity becomes the official religion of the Roman Empire, and the church attempts to stamp out pagan practices, which it calls heresies.
960	A church document states it is the duty of priests to "instruct the people that [belief in witchcraft is] absolutely untrue and that such imaginings are planted in the minds of misbelieving folk, not by a Divine spirit, but by the spirit of evil."
1229	The Inquisition, which had been started by the Roman Catholic Church in 1184, becomes a permanent institution. The purpose of the Inquisition was to find and eliminate heresy, but it soon turns to rooting out and torturing anyone who continued to observe pagan rituals or engage in the use of folk magic for healing.

1486	*Malleus Maleficarum*, a handbook for recognizing and killing witches, is published. Although the book was soon officially condemned by the Christian church, it continued to be widely used in local witch hunts until the early 18th century.
1515	500 women accused of being witches are burned at the stake in Geneva, Switzerland.
1563	Queen Elizabeth I passes the first Witchcraft Acts in England, outlawing witchcraft and fanning the flames of the Great Witch Craze.
1692	The Salem Witch Trials leave over 200 people dead.
1735	A new Witchcraft Act in England makes it illegal for anyone to engage in witch hunts.
1878	A Massachusetts woman takes a man to court for "mesmerizing" her in Salem. The case is thrown out.
1921	Margaret Murray's book *The Witch-Cult in Western Europe* promotes the theory that an ancient pagan cult of witches had survived in Europe until the witch trials of the 17th century.
1939	Gerald Gardner is initiated into witchcraft in the New Forest coven in England. During the 1940s and 1950s, Gardner developed many of the teachings that would become known as Wicca.
1974	The Council of American Witches agrees on the 13 "Principles of Wiccan Belief."
1975	The Covenant of the Goddess, a large organization of Wiccans and covens, is formed.
1986	Wicca is legally recognized by the U.S. government as a religion.
2008	A study shows that the number of American Wiccans had doubled since 2001.

GLOSSARY

amulet—an object used for protection against evil spirits or demons.

athame—a knife, usually a dagger, used in Wiccan rituals.

coven—a group of witches.

demonology—the study of demons.

Druid—a Celtic priest.

esbat—a non-sabbat gathering of Wiccans, usually during the full moon.

goetia—a form of low magic practiced in ancient Greece.

hekau—an ancient Egyptian magician.

incantation—a chant or spell that uses words.

initiation—a ritual in which a new witch enters a coven.

magi—a high magician or priest in ancient Greece and Rome.

magick—the use of a ritual or spell to create change. The archaic spelling is intended to differentiate it from the tricks and illusions of stage magicians.

mass hysteria—a situation in which a group of people exhibit irrational beliefs or behaviors.

neopagan—a person who practices paganism in the modern world.

New Age—a modern quasi-religious movement combining inclusive practices like astrology, paganism, and alternative medicine.

pentacle—a talisman featuring a five-pointed star.

rede—counsel or advice.

rune—an ancient Norse alphabet.

Sabbat—a Wiccan holy day.

spell—a sequence of magical words. See also: Incantation

theurgy—a form of high magic practiced in ancient Greece.

Wicca—a modern, Earth- and witchcraft-based religion. *See also* Neopagan.

witch hunt—an effort to find and root out witches.

Further Reading

Adler, Margot. *Drawing Down the Moon: Witches, Druids, Goddess-Worshippers, and Other Pagans in America Today*. Boston: Beacon Press, 1986.

Blake, Deborah. *Everyday Witch Book of Rituals: All You Need for a Magickal Year*. Woodbury, Minn.: Llewellyn Publications, 2012.

Bradley, Kris. *Mrs. B's Guide to Household Witchery: Everyday Magic, Spells, and Recipes*. San Francisco: Weiser Books, 2012.

Cunningham, Scott, and Kimberly Nightingale. *Wicca: A Guide for the Solitary Practitioner*. Woodbury, Minn.: Llewellyn Publications, 2011.

Guiley, Rosemary E. *The Encyclopedia of Witches, Witchcraft and Wicca*. New York: Checkmark Books, 2008.

Manoy, Lauren, and Yan Apostolides. *Where to Park Your Broomstick: A Teen's Guide to Witchcraft*. New York: Fireside Book, 2002.

RavenWolf, Silver. *To Ride a Silver Broomstick: New Generation Witchcraft*. St. Paul, Minn.: Llewellyn, 2008.

Starhawk. *The Spiral Dance: A Rebirth of the Ancient Religion of the Great Goddess*. San Francisco: HarperSanFrancisco, 1999.

INTERNET RESOURCES

http://paganwiccan.about.com

A huge collection of information, resources, and blogs about Wicca and witchcraft.

http://video.nationalgeographic.com/video/uk_wicca

A documentary about Wiccans in the UK.

http://salem.lib.virginia.edu/home.html

This electronic collection maintained by the University of Virginia has documents, resources, and historical information about the Salem Witch Trials.

www.english-heritage.org.uk/daysout/properties/stonehenge

Information about visiting Stonehenge in England.

www.cog.org

A place to get more information and read more about The Covenant of the Goddess, one of the oldest Wiccan organizations in the United States.

INDEX

Numbers in ***bold italic*** refer to captions.

About the Author

Audrey Alexander is not a witch. Her award-winning nonfiction has taken her to 1840s England, 1940s Amsterdam, and ancient Greece. She has lived in Massachusetts, California, Colorado and Germany. When she's not curled up with a book, you'll find her roller-skating, singing, or working on the perfect green chile stew.

PHOTO CREDITS: Library of Congress: 22, 24, 29, 30, 50; used under license from Shutterstock, Inc.: 3, 6, 10, 15, 18, 19, 34, 36, 38, 42, 43, 45, 47, 48, 51; 1000 Words / Shutterstock.com: 8, 9, 11; AISA-Everett/Shutterstock: 14, 23; Baciu / Shutterstock.com: 17; Littleny / Shutterstock.com: 28; Maisna / Shutterstock.com: 41; Sergemi / Shutterstock.com: 35; Wikimedia Commons: 25, 26, 32, 33.